This book is dedicated to **myself.**
If nothing else, at least, I have this.

Even when you are **lost**....

Lost & Found

by Michel M. Antoine

iiPUBLISHING

Lost & Found
Copyright © 2021 by Michel M. Antoine

Copyright notice
All rights reserved. No part of this book may be reproduced in any form or by any electronic or mechanical means, including information storage and retrieval systems, without permission in writing from the author or publisher, except for the use of brief quotations in a book review.

Cover design by tonii

ISBN: 978-1-7362167-4-3

Printed in the United States of America

iiPUBLISHING

New York, NY
www.toniiinc.com

You can **find** yourself again.

LOST | *three*

SEARCHING | *twenty-one*

FOUND | *fifty-one*

CONTENTS

Finding self-love through a journey of heartbreak, self-doubt, and insecurities

LOST

She was a puppet.
The master of approval unwittingly reigned all control.
She was a TV show. (Specifically, a sitcom.)
She needed laughter to make her feel better.
She hoped you'd stick around long enough to just
...
Watch
...
Listen
...
She was a flower
That died too quick because she wasn't picked....

How was *she* supposed to know
It was the sunshine of her ancestors,
The rain showers of Mother Nature
That was supposed to help her grow?
How was *she* supposed to know
That her **silence** actually meant something?
That for those who cared for her, it was deafening?
How was *she* supposed to know
That she was actually worthy?
Where did that come from?
Where did **she** come from?

She served as a **buffer**...

The line from point A to point B.
Settling somewhere in between his
"I wanna get married one day...
But not today."
She was the space between the rock and the hard place.
The gray in black and white movies.
Her smile lessened the tension
In any room she walked in
But, like clockwork, exploded behind closed doors
If the pressure persisted.
She lost herself, empowering others.
Pouring her soul into anyone who'd make her smile.
"Smile!" they'd say, when they saw her frown.
If only they saw how many times, she blamed herself,
For the cracks in the mirror and not those
Who broke it.
Accountability, she befriended.
Others scurried, becoming distant strangers.
She served as a goalie, blocking intrusions to her heart.
Stunned when they scored, as if her pore-filled
Gentleness wasn't already visible.
It was only a matter of time...
To be broken
Again.

She served as a buffer.
                    It was too wearisome
                                      To just be

                                                      Herself.

She sulked in a misery
That reeked
Of detriment to her soul.

> Replayed a song
> Until the tears began to roll.

> She became stuck and frozen
> By her own static choice.

> Submerged and suffocating
> From her own toxic decision.

> Her decision to dive in
> Became a painful blur.

>> Drowning,
>> She recalled,
>> She never knew
>> **How to swim.**

Raindrops
Splattered
Against the patio door
As desires for running off somewhere...........anywhere
Crystallized.
She idealized utopia:
Not being bothered by humans,
Yet a ceaseless battle remained.
She felt empowered by others
Alive and intimate
But the exigency to be alone
Bit deep.
She marveled in this moment
Hoping the present
Would give her the answers
She desperately
Needed.

Her mind raced like Wile E. Coyote
Running on roads towards the worst-case scenarios
Runnin' on dunkin' into hoops of failure
She was depleted before even beginning.

Her heart was nearly an erupting volcano
Hotter than the heat-filled vent
The anxious lava that spewed, burned everyone near
She begged for a different atmosphere.

Her soul was, an unclear black hole
Longing to be filled with clarity.
She was never aligned, a clown with a smile
A joke she felt glued to.

She necessitated more.
She couldn't just be
OK with all this noise.
She needed some peace, something different from she
She sought it in

Relationships.

How many **relationships** must she lose
To find the one?
The one that won't leave.
The "Kizzy" to her dreams.

She dreamed
And he
Appeared.
She believed
This
To be real.
She **lost** hope
And **found** it
In him.
She knew
They
Were meant...

...Whether meant
To be,
Spent
To breathe,
Bent
Out of shape,
Misaligned
With a dent,
Heartbreaks
Never hurt
Any less.

The first night away from him was the hardest...
She hoped.
There was an insistent thought of him
In everything she did.
His presence coated her mind but
She wasn't ready to **break free**.
She made a home
In his unforgiving mental prison.

Was it *her* that surpassed his limited expectations?

Was it him that drove past her ideal image?

Was it them misaligning like stars in constellations?

A universe apart with **polar** distant destinations?

What if all he was,
Was an aching pain in her heart,
A time-bomb, tick-tocking from the start,
An explosion of emotions,
Only to be with the aftermath
That **she + him**
Don't add up right?

She weighed her options,
Added her blessings,
Subtracted the vampires who sucked out her energy,
She divided her goals, matched them with the right Environment,
Multiplied abundance and sat…
And **waited**…

"I don't think I'm ready,"
A voice whispered.

She looked around,
Fear-stricken,
When no one else was present.
Was it her heart
That burned with compassion?
Was it her soul
That seeped in a grounding presence?
Was it her mind
That fluttered quick like butterfly wings?
She returned to her journal and pen, confused.
She wrote and wrote and wrote and wrote
And dedicated her next piece to
Words.

Dear words,
You are

.
.
.
.
.
.
.
.
.
.
.
.
.
.
.
.
.
.
.
.
.
.
.
.
.
.
.
.
.

HEAVY
Sometimes, *I* am not strong enough to carry.

SEARCHING

Write for yourself.
Write for me...
Write for the child buried deep inside,
The one that parted long ago.
When did you mature?
When were you considered an adult?
Was it 18?
Was it 7?
Are you still trying to figure out what that means?

Write for yourself.
Write for me.
STOP trying to share only your most precious parts!
I'm sorry...
Do you sense my aggression?
It's really quite passive.
Quite contradictory
To how I've been described.

I've been a tightrope walker
For as long as I can remember.
Left foot, compassion.
Right foot, confidence.
Left foot, stay kind.
Right foot, assertion...no, aggression!
I'm losing my balance!
I'm falling...
My stomach
Flies out my mouth!
My hands grasp exactly
What I feel on the inside...
Nothing.
I'm left

Left

Left

To **surrender.**

I looked for life in your text...

...Instead I was met
With sunflowers (my screensaver)
And a message box with no new numbers.
I looked for answers in your voice.
Instead your words spoken
Were like daggers to my thoughts,
Stabbing my creativity,
My feelings,
My ideas,
My everything.
I bled my power of autonomy to help you feel useful.
Dignified blood gushed out of me
As if I didn't really need it.
As if he was the one that kept me breathing.

He wasn't.

He won't
Rob me of my power any longer nor
Subjugate my rights and my uniqueness.
What I need...
Is not always easy to answer.
But I know in the depths of me...
Under French-vanilla skin infested with insecurity,
Behind wide smiles and constant laughs,
Crying for help,
Beneath greeting texts pleading for
Intimate connections,
There is a warmth only found in divine souls,
A heart so immense and warm,
It is the sun's only competition,
And a smile that lasts for light years,
It almost
Almost
Feels
                Like it's **genuine**.

To be **genuine**, honest, authentic, open,
We must face our most gruesome truths.

I callously swept the trauma beneath the rug,
But the particles got stuck…
To the broom
Then, stuck
To my feet.
As I tried to efface
The fault and shame off my hands
From the effort in removing them from my soles
I noticed,
With more gentle strokes,
With unrelenting patience,
I no longer needed to rigorously
Wash away the memories
To my whole and complex being.
The memories that make me, me.

I'm being **present.**
And waiting…

Speak to me.
Tell me the answers.
Stop running away when I haven't yet grasped it.
Slow down a bit.
You're speaking too fast.
I process things slow.
You'll need some patience.

>Patiently wait
>As my emotions run wild
>**Like a wilderness beast**
>Tugging at your heartstrings.
>They'll nibble on your core
>And twist your insides.
>My heart falls like led, ricochets off my body.
>Your eyes become the sun
>As my skin melts away.

I'm still waiting for an answer.
Some kind of guidance.
At least point out
Which direction to go in.

> **Self-love,** they call it?
> Sounds unattainable.
> What does it look like?
> It feels **unusual**.

> Just start walking,
> They say.
> Left foot first.
> That way if you fall,
> You'll be right on time.

Do you know what it feels like
To be three steps off?
I'm running **out of breath**
Trying to be like everyone else.

My mannerisms are polite.
I'm told I'm awkward.
I've learned to say thank you
When I'm referred to as weird.

I won't get the answer
From anyone else,
So **here I go**
In attempts to loving myself:

I am destined for greatness.

I am destined for greatness.

I am destined for greatness.

I am destined for greatness.

Greatness...
Didn't come easily.
It dabbled in accomplishments,
Goals that were set and met.
It fiddled in the mirror on good hair days.
It puttered in moments, never long-standing.
Relaxing, **just being,** was still not OK.

OK, I will not be a buffer…**I will not** be a buffer…

I'm still trying to find **my purpose**....

...You'd think by all the thorns of anxiety,
Depression,
Heartbreak,
Failure,
That I could no longer blossom.

But my dear, have you ever seen anything perfect
Without a crack,
A bend,
A dent?
I haven't.
It takes a storm to see a rainbow,
Pressure to form a diamond,
The deepest of pains
To birth songs that will last forever.
I don't know why I'm here nor how I got here.
But I am.
Here.
And I know
That when music takes over my body,
When I sit in a bed of grass,
When I write
& read
& hug
& laugh,
I know
I'm supposed
To be here.

But still He…
>   Penetrates my mind intrusively
>   > Without asking
>   > > Breaking down a mental cage twistedly,

I feel more safe in
Locked up,
>   Away from him.

I chalk up this choke up
>   To life.
>   > The way it split down
>   > > **A crooked line**
>   > > > Of love
>   > > > > And lust.

Balancing the two
Got me dizzy, love struck, and sick.
>   > > Wishing my heart wasn't as big.

That it would save me,
Not hurt me.
They never save me.
>   > >ND They always hurt me.

I'm running out of room
To put Band-Aids on.
>   There's a warrior in there
>   > Somewhere.
>   > > I promise.

I'm holding on with all my might.
>   Fighting
>   > For my dear life.

Dear life,
She isn't done yet.

Dear love,
She is just getting started.

Dear heart,
Don't give up yet.

Dear soul,
Her saving grace.
Save her from the wounds,
From the clarity others could not yet see,
The wisdom others have not yet gained,
The respect others never learned,
The emotions that were not validated,
The warmth others did not receive.

Dear self,
Love is knocking.
She promises to be kind.
Respectful.
Patient.
Patient.
Patience, my dear.
You are healing.

It's been seven days with a dab of forever.

The flood gates haven't yet opened
But it seems I walk with a weight I didn't ask for.
As if each heartbreak is a link
In a massive chain of defeat.
I'm not sure how much longer I can survive with the
Wind knocked out of me...
Loss
After **loss**
After **loss**
Simultaneously
Finding myself
After
Each one.
As if I **lose** myself in these relationships,
I try
To find
Myself.
I am often blinded,
Stuck in a fog of desperate approval.
Constantly looking around, rather than
Within.
My penmanship
Has always taken a liking to the words: I love you.
A couple years ago, I replaced you for me.
I've been trying to live that way ever since…

I love me.

I love me.

I love me.

I love me.

I love me.

I love me.

I love me.

My mind coiled around an unfamiliar
But empowering image.
A woman, a bada** who had her sh*t together!
She stood tall, about 5'6.
Her face emulated her hearts expressions.
She was in tune with herself,
Radiating with confidence.
She forgave herself...accepting bad things happen.
She accepted her flaws and used them to her advantage
To prepare, to plan ahead, to love herself...

As is.

I love you hung onto the awkward silence
Like a branch yearning to fall.
To **rebirth** into its grounding roots.
To be told this is where you belong.
To be told there is nothing to fear
When love
Is present.

I love you.

- Self-reflection

There is a tender blossoming
That is unraveling
That I don't want to touch
For fear
My fingerprints
Will destroy
The image **that is hidden.**
It is no mirage, but it feels big
And closer
Than it really is.
For once,
I am OK,
Yes, *I* am OK…
With taking my time
To get there.

-Self-love

When I struggle to find the love within,
I find it in:

The air I breathe in.

The water I bathe in.

The ground I walk on.

The fork my lips kiss.

The brush that caresses my hair, gently.

The brush that cleanses my teeth, securely.

The mirror that receives my wide smile.

The blanket that keeps me warm at night.

The clothes that rest placidly on my body.

I place my right hand on my chest.
I listen to the beat that was made just for me
I really listen…
To

My heartbeat.

Dear Cheli,

Do you realize how much I've **missed you**?
I've longed for your creativity,
The way your heart burns with passion, with love,
With an ever so graceful touch, with a yearning to be
Accepted, and to love
Wholeheartedly.

FOUND

What I came here to receive is:
                Expression,
           A moment of stillness,
                 To reflect,
                To quiet down,
                 To release,
          To let go of the tension
                  Between
      My   Shoulders.
What I came here to receive is:
                Acceptance,
                  Love,
                   Joy,
                  Peace.
I came here to be with me again.

What I came here to receive are:
    The gifts I often bury for fear of being judged.
      I came here for guidance and support.
          Sometimes, I need a push.

I came here to **retrieve**:
        The strength in my voice,
    Combatting the screaming lies in the mirror.
        The power in my step,
      Grounding yet trembling beneath me.
        The song in my heart,
      That dies and lives again like cats.
        The unity of all of me,
          Body, soul, and mind.

I am creativity.
I have a troubled time finding where creation ends,
And I begin.
I am movement.
I rise
And
Fall to the rhythm of my own heartbeat.
Ideas swim through me with different
Colors, sh▲pes, siz$e$s, forms.
I don't always know where masterpieces go...

...but they often peacefully land
On pages
Like these.

These words will always find the answers.

When my fragile, intense heart pops out my chest like Jack in the Box,

When thick boulders lay on my throat,

When my brain's lightbulb turns on,
Landing on the perfect articulation to my feelings…
It's always too late.

These words save me from going under.

These words
Are always
On time.

But every now *and* then…

I wrote about everything under the sun
And still didn't feel warm.
I thought of the moon
That cries wolf,
Begs for attention.
How selfish…
And uniquely
Beautiful.

Who is it that determines
What's considered a "problem"?
No matter how daunting,
Let's give some space to not knowing…
To figuring
It out.
After all, we are concurrently
Masterpieces
And
Works in progress.

As we progress,
We steep,
Marinate in time,
With no rush…
No rush.

We sip unhurriedly,
Let it linger on our tongues…
All five senses,
A magnet to the present,
Omnipresent warmth.

We treasure the moment,
That tomorrow doesn't promise,
Finding joy in each slow breath.

We embrace vitality,
Jettison brutality.
We, the prized possessions, are found…

In mirrors
And moments
And touches
And breaths
And heartbeats
And
Just being.

Just being, but muted
By fears, misperceptions, misunderstandings, doubt,
And feeling incapable.

Just being, and reminding myself
Minds are stunning, intelligent,
And divine in their own right.

Just being, and knowing
The approval of others should never be required
To embrace magic
Laced in veins,
Beating out hearts.

Just being, and remembering
To express...
To articulate the thoughts,
I think everyone has the answer to.
They don't.
Not in my voice, at least.

Just being, I'll remember
I am special.
Exceptional.
I am who I think I am.

Today,
I
Am
Dynamite.

I exploded

With

Warmth

Gratitude

Abundance

A sanctuary

A home

That was there

All along.

A longing reflection
Became more clear

I looked in the **mirror**
Y tenía estos pensamientos:

I've wanted to write about your face for some time.
The way it **contours** into a lifetime.
The way your scent cradles me with comfort, stability,
Forever, and then some.
The way your eyes tell a story:
I've been here, right here, this whole time.

- Self-reflection

But judgement started peering...

Judgement, I am no longer
Allowing you to take control

You no longer have power.

Have you not witnessed the dynamite that seeps
Through my bones?
The fire in my heart?
The creation
Written
All over me?

Judgement, every time you come around,
I will look you in the eye and remind you of the years
I've taken you down
I have accomplished so much
I have beat you at **your own game**
I have won time and time again
I am the conductor and passenger
Of my journey of life
I will continue to express myself,
Reminding myself of my worth.

Judgment, I am now here without you...

Thriving, soaring, as free as a bird
As loud as a rainforest
As vicious as a lion
As fierce as a wolf,
A she-wolf.

Nothing less.

Everything more.

Nothing less.

Everything more.

More,
More,
More,
More, and
At the most
I found
My highest
Self…

Letter from my **Higher Self**:

My dearest Michel,

Before you go, please know, firstly, that I am never far.
All you must do is continue
To venture on this path called life,
And I will wait for you.
Secondly, you are not alone, and never will be.
My translucent spirit painted with pink, purple, and
Blue hues will await your presence.
It is with large wings she stands.
Holding close to her heart, your dreams,
And shooing away
Any doubt you come across.
My dearest Michel,
Now to get to my lessons, as you know I speak with
Intention and sometimes the most
Important lessons are found in the journey.

Here they are:

1. Follow your heart.

2. Your spirit is warm.

3. Your nature is kind.

4. There is nothing you are not capable of.

1. Follow your heart.

2. Your spirit is eternal.

3. Your nature is kind.

4. There is and has you are not capable of

I am the cliffhanger I don't mind falling from.
I am sure I will land into a sea of love,
An ocean of comfort.
I will be moved by waves of passion,
An uncertain certainty,
A calming aura, and
A soothing voice of reason.
Here, I am seen.
I am heard,
And
With poetry.
It is why I
Continue to write.
My voice,
Like the ocean,
Kissing the horizon
And the endless possibilities of my abilities to
Soar.

I am flying.

I thank myself
Just as much as I do...
Poetry.

AFTERWORD

Even when you are lost, you can find yourself again. I have lost myself many times in life, and everytime I return, there is something grand, something unwritable, something... that happens... and I fall in love with myself on a deeper level all over again. My message to you is to never stop doing for yourself. In moments where I have felt lost, I realized that I was often giving too much to others when I did not have the space or energy to. I needed to look within. There, is where I often found the answers of exactly what I needed. We cannot pour from an empty cup. When we give more space to love ourselves, we naturally give space for others to do the same. Prioritize yourself. Prioritize your needs. You will never lose yourself if you are constantly giving. Treat yourself like an everlasting blooming flower and give yourself the soil, the sun, and the water that you need to grow.

In this journey of finding myself and my purpose, I hope to continue creating. I hope that on this journey, I create more written pieces, and that our paths align once again.

Stay tuned for more to come.

THE AUTHOR

MICHEL M. ANTOINE

Michel M. Antoine writes with her heart. Her emotions drive her, and her pen has saved her. She has been writing since a child and released her first book in 2018. "STOP, LOVE, & LISTEN" is a self-published collection of poems and journal entries that explores self-love, following intuition, and being present in life. Michel's experience in writing began with journaling and later, she ventured into poetry. Michel uses writing as a form of artistic expression and self-healing and encourages others to do the same. Outside of writing, Michel is a Bilingual Licensed Mental Health Counselor, dancer, and certified Zumba instructor. You can find more information about her at:

www.MichelTherapy.com

www.ingramcontent.com/pod-product-compliance
Lightning Source LLC
Chambersburg PA
CBHW072207100526
44589CB00015B/2410